BLESSED
BY THE
NIGHT

BLESSED BY THE NIGHT

BY MARK LAURENSON

Published by Mark Laurenson
Warsaw, Indiana 46580
ISBN-13: 978-1491082072
ISBN-10: 1491082070

Cover and interior design by Terry Julien
Contributing author/editor: Hillary Burgardt
Some names have been changed at the request of participants in the story

Printed in the United States of America

What Others are Saying About This Book

"In sobriety we are called to share 'our experience, strength and hope.' Mark truly exemplifies these characteristics. His is a story of despair, courage and triumph. He is one of the most compelling people I have had the privilege of working with. He is an inspiration to all of us who are in recovery."

John Mcclanahan, Phd., CCDC, LCADC
Addiction Counselor
McClanahan & Associates

"Mark Laurenson's testimony beautifully parallels the utter depravity of addiction with the awesome power and tenacity of God's love. As a clinician and Christian, his story reminds me that no man's circumstances are beyond God's ability to heal and to redeem for His glory."

Dr. Bruce Turnquist
Psychologist

"Mark Laurenson has a profound way of communicating to all types of audiences. I have personally witnessed him effectively reach many people with his life-changing testimony. I highly recommend Mark to share his story."

Jamie Clark, M.A.
Former Counselor
Teen Challenge

"Mark Laurenson wisely observes, 'Troubles can be our friends and a sign that God is paying attention to us. Welcome them as the gift God intended them to be.' Here is the moving story of a man who may have felt forgotten by his fellow man, but he was not forgotten by his God. God was paying attention to Mark all along his painful journey, shaping him and molding him to trust Christ more strongly and reflect Christ more brightly."

Larry E. McCall, D. Min.
Pastor of Christ's Covenant Church
Author of *Walking Like Jesus Did*

WITH DEEPEST GRATITUDE

Bryan and Stephen Laurenson

Marie

Harry and JoEllen Valentine

Joel Pautsch

The staff of Christ's Covenant Church

And my life partner, Robin Laurenson

Special thanks to Terry White

FOREWORD

During the past several decades, Dr. D. James Kennedy has been a champion of the faith. His defense of America is surpassed only by his bold and insightful preaching.

I once got to hear him speak on why Jesus picked Peter. He spent most of his time reflecting on Peter's passion to mess things up! The sermon's ending was short and powerful, a trademark of most of Dr. Kennedy's sermons.

So why was Peter picked over everyone else? It was because Jesus noticed that as quick as Peter was to sin, he was even quicker to repent. In fact Peter's ability to identify his sin and repent from it made him a leader among his peers. Peter's deep regret for his sin often led him to "weep bitterly" in public for those sins (Matthew 26:75).

Dr. Kennedy closed with ten powerful words: "Have you wept for your sin? If you haven't, *you will*."

It was Peter's example that opened the door for my own heart to see Jesus clearly and made it possible for me to weep for my own sin. When we see our own sin we are moved to follow Christ. This book would never have been written without the Holy Spirit's guidance!

CONTENTS

INTRODUCTION

In the movie "Same Time, Next Year" Johnny Mathis sang a song that dramatically caught my attention. He, along with songstress Jane Oliver, reflected:

"Dreams make promises they cannot keep . . . "

When I was five I dreamed of being a soldier. At ten I wanted to be a pilot. Not just any pilot, but the best, the "rocket men" who ventured to the high desert of California to a mythical place called Edwards Air Force Base. To be dropped from 52,000 feet from the belly of a B-52, hear the five seconds of utter silence, then hear and feel the raw power of four unfettered rocket engines launching me toward the edges of space. Yeager, Crossfield, Laurenson . . . ah, if only I wasn't afraid of heights!

When I was 12 my parents gave me my first real cool pencil. They called it a mechanical pencil that architects used. My only orders in church were to sit still, be quiet and draw something with that nifty pencil! Now I knew I was born to be an architect, a dream I pursued for the next decade of my young life.

I never became a solider or a rocket pilot or even an architect. Back then I believed it was about becoming something that made life meaningful. I later discovered that what counted most was what I was becoming on the inside.

I just never imagined the costs involved in that journey nor did I ever envision the peace and joy that would be my reward.

Chapter One

Scotland
THE STREETS OF MY ANCESTORS

As the train pulled out of Glasgow, the city slipped quickly from view. The beauty of the Scottish countryside, the lush rolling hills, quiet hamlets and grazing lambs seemed like something out of a medieval romance novel. Apart from the entrancing loveliness of its scenery, Scotland is historically distinguished by both its romance and violence. My visit to Stirling two days earlier had taken me back to a time when William Wallace and warring Scots marched to the haunting sound of bagpipes.

Arriving in Edinburgh, I was transported into the world of my ancestors. A second generation Scot, I had grown up with stories of the old country. Now I was walking the streets where once my grandparents had held hands and dreamed of their life to come in the new world. The sights and sounds of that ancient city made me feel as though I had come home. I had somehow made contact with my past. I thought perhaps it would give me hope for tomorrow. It did not.

My profession had provided my transportation from the U.S. to this far land. Various forms of educational publishing had entitled me to a level of recognition. That had, in turn, afforded me an invitation to share my thoughts at the annual conference of the International Facilities Managers Association. I was honored to be there. It seemed like a fitting capstone to my 30-year career. I had no idea how final that moment in time would be.

It appeared I was riding high that June day in 2000; a handsome income, two loving sons, a marriage of twenty-three years, a four-bedroom home in a desirable neighborhood in Annapolis, Maryland, and two new cars in the driveway. I coached T-ball and served in my church. I should have been on top of the world. But all was not as it seemed. My family and a few very close friends knew that my inner demons were closing in on me. In only four weeks, my life would plunge into a darkness that looked very much like a death spiral.

So how does someone flying so high crash and burn only to rise again? The answer to that question is in the pages that follow.

Chapter Two

Detroit
THE CENTER OF THE UNIVERSE

"Life can only be understood backwards;
but it must be lived forwards."

Soren Kierkegaard
Danish Philosopher

The year was 1946. World War II had just come to a dramatic end as the atomic age dawned over the skies of Japan. On the other side of the world, Detroit, Michigan, was busy converting itself into the greatest industrial complex the world had ever seen. People around the world knew the city of Detroit to be the place where the great American middle class was being born.

To look at it today, it is hard to believe that Detroit and its surrounding areas were once a place of great vitality and vision. As the nation's fifth largest city, Detroit was the place to be. New York's Macys may have had the country's largest Thanksgiving Day Parade but Detroit's J.L Hudson Company had the nation's second largest. The Ford River Rouge factory was the largest in the world, and the Ford Rotunda was as magical a place as the early '50s had to offer. The Rotunda was first used at the 1936 World's Fair in Chicago. Moved to Detroit in the early '50s, it served as Ford's world headquarters, and, more importantly to me, as a fantasyland at Christmas and Easter. At the time, it was the nation's fifth most visited vacation attraction.

That was the world I was born into on October 27, 1946, to Thomas and Dorothy Laurenson. Thomas, the son of a Scottish immigrant, was the youngest of three children. He was raised in Cleveland and attended Purdue University just before the outbreak of World War II. Dorothy Cameron was one of eight children born to Zee and Betty Cameron. Nebraska farmers, they moved to Detroit in the '30s to make their fortune in the auto factories, which offered big paychecks to those who would work hard. You may wonder what kind of name Zee is. Well as the story goes he was the last of eighteen children. His parents seemed to want to make a statement that that was going to be it as far as children went.

My father was a junior, named after his father, Thomas Malcolm Laurenson. I never knew my grandfather, but I was told he was a staunch Presbyterian. He was stern but not mean in any way. He and my grandmother immigrated to America when they were sixteen. They were actually Shetlanders, having been born and raised on one of the most remote spots on earth, the Shetland Islands. The Islands are windswept dots in the North Atlantic. According to family history neither of them had ever seen a tree higher than four feet tall until they arrived in the United States. My grandfather was a hard-working man who owned his own grocery store in Cleveland. He died of a heart attack one Sunday morning while singing a hymn in church. My father had some of his own father's characteristics, but for the most part he was gentle and kind, strong in body and character.

My father was, by all respects, a self-made man. Expecting to be drafted, he left Purdue and moved to Detroit to make a little money while he waited. As it turned out, his company was declared important to the war effort, and he was given a deferment for the length of the war. His salary was 12 cents an hour, meager by any standards. After the war, his company encouraged loyal employees to stay on. By the time he died, my dad was viewed by his peers as the go-to man when it came to titanium welding and manufacturing. Titanium was a space age metal, and through self-education my father became an expert on the topic as well as an author.

It was not his work that made him special, but rather his character. He was full of life. From helping friends build houses to hooking up chimes for the neighborhood church, dad seemed to be everywhere. I fondly remember his basement workshop where dozens of Junior Achievement hopefuls churned out products, mostly memo pads, to sell and make their mark in the community. At his funeral scores of people bowed at his casket, some sobbing. Many of them I never knew. My mother later told me some of their stories. My father had helped every one of them.

My mother was a stay-at-home mom. She never drove a car. She never ran for PTA president. She simply cared for her household, which mostly consisted of me since I was an only child. She was faithful, loving and devout. She was always there when I needed her, and she taught me well. On one occasion I remember her overhearing me use a four-letter word. She summoned me to the house. Fearing a warm bottom was in my immediate future, I slowly closed the front door behind me. Her lesson was not physical. She simply and sternly said, "Anyone can use bad language. You are not just anybody. Start acting accordingly." To this day, her words echo through my brain whenever someone curses.

I WAS ONLY ELEVEN YEARS OLD BUT I WAS GOING TO HAVE TO GROW UP IN A HURRY.

During the war, mom worked for the government. One of her responsibilities was to find qualified workers for a top-secret placement. She would find out afterward that she had helped staff an isolated operation in rural Tennessee. Oak Ridge Laboratories was a major player in developing the atomic bombs dropped on Japan and continues today as a major player in producing atomic materials.

Detroit was the motor capital of the world in the '50s. Family lore has it that my first word was Pontiac. I seriously doubt that was true, but "car" was a real possibility. We were not rich, but our needs were few. It was an idyllic world.

All that changed one cold December afternoon. As I walked home from the bus stop after school, I noticed a flurry of activity around our home – lots of cars and the unnerving sight of an ambulance parked in our driveway. I was only eleven years old but I was going to have to grow up in a hurry, as I learned that my father had suffered a severe heart attack. It was an event serious enough to kill him, serious enough to permanently damage his heart. It was a life-altering event for my mother and for me as well.

It is hard to recall all my feelings that day, but fear and confusion would be a good starting place. I didn't know it at the time, but my "Leave it to Beaver" world was about to come crashing down. My first blessing of the night was about to begin.

My father's sudden fall from health to the fringes of life was dramatic. The day of the heart attack he weighed 170 pounds. Three weeks later he was down to below 120. Over the next ten years we spent seven Christmases by his side in the hospital. At that time the number one TV show was *Dr. Kildare*. The theme song, "Three Stars Will Shine," still competes in my mind with traditional music. As I watched my father fight the battle of his life I noticed how it changed him. Not just physically, but in character. Where once he helped people with their electrical, plumbing, and woodworking problems, he now engaged them at a different level, their emotions. He became a counselor to many, taking action when necessary. He bore their secret burdens and sometimes their sins.

PAIN AND DESPAIR HAD RESHAPED MY FATHER INTO A VESSEL THAT HELPED REPAIR SOULS.

At his funeral, scores of men came to his casket and wept uncontrollably. For the most part I barely knew their names. As they came, my mother explained how dad had touched their lives. I still feel a need to protect their privacy, although one story may give some insight. One day after work, a man dad worked with came home to discover his house and family had all perished in a fire. The man was overcome with grief, as you can imagine. The grief did not subside but worsened, and the man became a recluse. Dad determined to stop by every day after work and deliver him a paper or magazine. He then, as the man allowed, would go inside for a brief chat. Day after day, month after month, dad was faithful, and the relationship grew. Eventually, after more than a year, the man found the strength to move on with his life. He was one of the men sobbing at the foot of dad's casket. Pain and despair had reshaped my father into a vessel that helped repair souls instead of household issues.

In later years, I would realize that watching my father handle his deepest of waters taught me more about character and what it meant to be a man than the good years ever had.

Chapter Three

Being a Teenager
DEALING WITH SICKNESS

As dad's lot in life became clear, another calamity was brewing. When I was thirteen a sudden pain began to plague my lower back. It was serious enough to put me in the emergency room several times a year. The doctors said it was nerves and that I was just upset about my father. As time passed there would be periods of little problems followed by the mysterious onset of severe pain. My parents took me to every doctor they could get to see me. At one point, I was admitted to the famous Ford Hospital in Detroit. The results were always the same, no evident problem. This curse lasted through college and into my second year of seminary.

I had started college in Detroit with the dream of becoming an architect, but as my relationship with the Lord grew a different path became apparent. I transferred to Grace College and Theological Seminary in Winona Lake, Indiana, and began to study speech, communication, and the Bible. In 1969 I began seminary there after finishing my bachelor's degree. All the while my pain continued and an unidentified problem was allowed to grow.

While returning to school in the fall of 1970, I collapsed getting out of my car and was rushed to a nearby hospital. A missionary doctor home on furlough was called. Without even coming in to see me, he listened to the same symptoms dozens of experts had heard before. With little hesitation he said that it sounded like a kidney problem, and he ordered tests to be administered. The next morning a gloomy medical staff gave me the news. I had a large mass in my left kidney, and judging from preliminary evaluations, it was likely a tumor that had been allowed to grow over the years. The doctors were grim, but I was ecstatic! I wasn't crazy. The pain wasn't psychosomatic; it had an identifiable, physical cause. My pain was real. It was decided that the kidney would need to be removed but the regional hospital near the school was not the place for such a procedure.

My mother and uncle arrived from Detroit quicker than I could learn all the names of the cute nurses! With little turn-around time allotted, I lay down in the back of Uncle Henry's station wagon. We went directly to the hospital where a medical team was waiting, and within 24 hours of my diagnosis, I was under the knife. The pain I had endured before seemed like child's play as I slowly awoke in the surgery recovery room. Kidney surgeons in the '60s seemed to have little tenderness as they cut through bone and muscle. I was given strong pain medication every four hours, but it seemed to only last about 20 minutes! For the next three hours I tried to behave as a man. I'm sure the medical staff felt I was someone much younger!

The surgery had saved my kidney or at least part of it. It had also saved my life. The doctors told me that my left kidney was in a state of disintegration caused by a massive kidney infection. They conjectured that I had another six to eight months before my body would have succumbed to the infections.

Keep in mind that it was now January in Indiana, and it was cold and grey and not a place that lifted my spirits. One day I got a call from a dear friend in Miami, Florida. The sunshine seemed to ooze through the wires. I was offered two choices 1) stay in Winona Lake and heal slowly or 2) I could catch the next flight to Miami! After a serious round of Hallelujahs, I composed myself enough to tell my friend, Dr. Larry Poland, that I would be there as soon as my doctors allowed. Hanging up the phone, I began to cry for joy. God had not only begun the healing of my body but had now directed me to the next step on my journey and had connected me with my first spiritual mentor, Dr. Larry Poland.

GOD HAD NOT ONLY BEGUN THE HEALING OF MY BODY BUT HAD NOW DIRECTED ME TO THE NEXT STEP.

I wish I could say my medical journeys were a thing of the past. But they were not. After over a decade of doctors' neglect I continued to deal with kidney infections.

I hope you will pay close attention to the next series of events because they changed many lives. I can take absolutely none of the credit!

Soon I was promoted to Director of Admissions at Miami Christian College. One of my responsibilities was to schedule traveling music groups and enjoy acting as chaperone and college spokesman. I had done this for three years, and it was a high point in my single life. Our group kicked off one particular tour by performing on a Monday morning in the college chapel. We were to then leave immediately for a three-week tour. The college radio station, WMCU, was there to cover the kick-off event live and to give us a proper send-off. As the moment approached for me to announce the group and introduce the first song, something was wrong. I was missing. The quiet mumblings began, "Where is Mark?"

WHILE I LAY SLEEPING, THE VERY ONE WHO CREATED ME WAS WORKING A MIRACLE.

The evening before our send-off had taken a surprising turn. Shortly after dinner with friends I had collapsed on the floor in my living room. Unconscious, I was rushed to the nearest hospital. By morning, mostly through the voice of our Christian radio station, the Christian community of South Florida knew things were not normal.

Several others took control of the group, since as they say, "The show must go on!" Our group, HISfolk, left on time that Monday morning, but I stayed behind. The concern over my health was growing.

It was my kidney, my left kidney. It was failing all of a sudden and my life had become uncertain. The surgeons had quickly decided that it must come out. But the doctors, good men all, did not realize that a Christian radio station had been broadcasting into thousands of homes of believers, and those prayers offered up on my behalf were backed by the power of the living God. He had the power to heal the sick and down-

---

14

hearted. While I lay sleeping, the very One who created me was working a miracle.

On Tuesday morning, with friends overloading the room praying for a miracle, my doctor walked in. I was barely awake but his words were unforgettable. "I did one last check this morning. You are going to make a believer of me yet. The problems are gone – they are just gone. Mark can go home as soon as he wants to!"

For months I got cards and letters from all over South Florida, most from individuals or families. I even got words of blessing from entire Christian school classes who had been praying for me because of the constant updates on WMCU. From Baptists to Presbyterians to the good folks at the Church of God, they didn't all believe alike, but they KNEW the same Creator and God.

Just for the record, I have never gotten another kidney infection!

Chapter Four

Annapolis
FINDING SUCCESS AND FINDING MY DEMONS

[This chapter was first published in 2004 as a single booklet under the title of "Testimony." It was distributed in connection with talks given to people beginning their journey to recovery from alcoholism and drug addiction.]

In the early '90s my body began to show signs of aging. Arthritic hands and feet slowed my pace, and constant lower back pain often made my days a never-ending search for relief. My doctors felt the solution was to be found in mild doses of pain medication. Tylenol #3 relieved the pain. It seemed like a miracle. I could function. I felt normal, even younger again. The years passed. A second son, a bigger house and career successes all increased my responsibilities and took me from boyhood to manhood. However, the journey that looked so easy on the outside slowly became Chinese water torture on the inside. More health issues assailed me. Glaucoma, psoriasis, and diabetes surrounded me like armies of advancing troops.

By this time I had started working for a company in Annapolis and it was only adding to my already numerous problems. Political wars and immorality and corruption at the highest levels of leadership brought a darkness to my soul that I had never before experienced. Though I had supporters at work and satisfaction in my job, the atmosphere had become a constant battle against a coworker who made trouble for me at every turn. It was not a healthy environment and that contributed to my deteriorating mental and physical health.

This is the part of the story where sin really made all the difference. Marie, my wife, suggested I quit my job to relieve some of the stress from my life. I had become comfortable, though. I liked my tidy income and big house, and though we could have been just as happy in an apartment I was unwilling to change. My lifestyle had made me greedy to keep it up, and because of that greed things were going to get much worse.

I LIKED MY TIDY INCOME AND BIG HOUSE. I WAS UNWILLING TO CHANGE.

Growing family problems provided little solace at the end of the day. Physical pain continued to assault my feelings of self worth, and the emotional pain drained all my hopes and dreams. Tylenol turned to Percocet. Percocet became Oxycontin. I was quickly discovering that these medications for physical pain also did wonders for my emotional pain. I had tumbled into the frightening world of addiction. I was an addict.

The soothing effects of narcotics quickly turned to panic. I was now taking anything I could get my hands on just to feel "normal." I knew I was in serious trouble, but I had no idea how to get out. Who could I turn to for help? Faith in God had always been a big part of my life. I was a true believer, but God now seemed so far off. For years my prayers for physical healing had seemed to go unanswered. Why would He pay attention now? I felt desperately alone.

In 2000, a few weeks after a work trip in Scotland, I checked into Father Martin's Ashley, a drug rehab facility. While I was there, my wife of 23 years left me. My sons didn't want to be near me. My church treated me as a leper. My job and my very career were less than a year from an untimely death. Hell may have more flames, but it couldn't be any lonelier than I felt.

THE DARK TIME OF MY OWN LIFE WAS NOT OVER.

The next two years became a blur. Day turned to night, night turned to day. I could hardly tell the difference. A few close friends eased the loneliness, but despair was always my companion, reminding me of my plight. In September of 2002, out of money and with little relief in sight, I packed the few belongings I had left and moved in with a total stranger. I thought things couldn't get any worse. I was wrong.

My time at Father Martin's did not progress as planned. With my poor eating and sleeping habits I was not healthy enough to move on to the second phase, but they let me stay there anyway. During my time I mentored other men through their struggles, but the dark time of my own life was not over.

Only ten days later, my life as I had known it came to a terrible end. While driving along the local interstate, reflexes slowed by years of drug abuse, I fell asleep. Traveling an estimated 90 miles an hour, I crashed violently into the median guardrail. When I woke in the hospital I had no memory of the

---

accident. One day later I walked out of the hospital with no significant injuries. The next day, I went to a previously scheduled doctor's appointment with my rheumatologist. After hearing of my ordeal and listening to my never-ending complaints of pain, he wrote me a prescription for 180 Percocet. I was suffering from both physical and emotional trauma, and I proceeded to consume inordinate quantities, nearly 180 pills in three days. The consequences were catastrophic. If the car accident didn't kill me, certainly this should have closed the lid on my casket.

I could hardly speak when I arrived at the hospital. My brain was barely functioning. I struggled to make sense of my situation. The hospital staff treated me like the scum I had become. I was a nameless drug addict to them, and they couldn't have been more uncaring. After only two days of detoxification, a true miracle in itself, it was time for me to go elsewhere. But where was I to go? My housemate of ten days didn't want anything to do with me. By this time my wife was remarried. My mother lived in a nursing facility. My friends had had enough. I was out of money. I was homeless. The only solution for the moment was to find shelter at yet another rehab center.

Warwick Manor is a drug and alcohol rehabilitation facility on the eastern shore of Maryland. Formerly a Baltimore Colts training center, it was in the middle of nowhere. What had kept the rambunctious football players at bay was appropriate for keeping sinners from getting out and saints from getting in. But I met some very special people there. They were people just like me, men and women who had accomplished many things with their lives; however, sobriety was not one of them. I truly wish

---

I could find them now to tell them how their concern for me helped. They seemed to sense my dire situation, and dire it was.

My time there was short. After only one week, I was informed that my insurance had run out and I would have to leave. Since I had nowhere to go, they were shipping me like a bag of groceries to a mental hospital in Baltimore. The van dropped me off at the front door and then vanished. I waited for seven hours to find a place for the night. Finally, I was told that they had no record of my coming and that it didn't matter anyway, because they didn't accept my insurance. They assured me, though, that I would be taken care of that night. They had a place for me to stay. A van appeared and took me to that place, a homeless shelter that had not yet opened for the night. I was left in an alley in the inner city of Baltimore, alone and frightened beyond belief.

> I WAS LEFT IN AN ALLEY IN THE INNER CITY OF BALTIMORE, ALONE AND FRIGHTENED BEYOND BELIEF.

I stood there watching the van disappear from sight, trying to comprehend what was happening to me. Nobody knew where I was, and even if they did, I was convinced that they couldn't have cared less. But I was wrong. The very God who knew me from before the creation of the world and counted the number of hairs on my head knew exactly where I was. What followed can only be explained as miraculous. What I am about to tell you is the truth. Nothing has been added. Nothing has been taken away.

As I turned and walked toward the lifeless hulk of a building I would call home for the night, a man appeared. He moved

---

from the shadow of the building and asked if I needed help. Help, I thought, was not what I needed; deliverance was more what I had in mind. He asked my name. "Mark," I replied. He offered that he also had been given the same biblical name. This simple coincidence briefly calmed my fears and allowed me the courage to share my situation. He told me not to worry; he would watch out for me.

During the day, homeless shelters are usually closed to the huddled masses. At night people seem to come out of the woodwork. The sight of all these gloomy men brought a new horror to my soul. How would I survive? Nothing in my white, affluent life had prepared me for this moment. I felt as though I had a giant bull's eye on my chest saying, "Mug me, hurt me." Then, in an indescribable way, my terror melted into numbness. My mind began to shut down. I struggled to make sense of my plight, but to no avail. I just could not rise to the occasion. It was Mark who came to my rescue. He stayed nearby, giving me advice, sensing I needed protection.

I FELT AS THOUGH I HAD A GIANT BULL'S EYE ON MY CHEST SAYING, "MUG ME, HURT ME."

As we climbed the stairs to the third floor, he showed me the ropes. Mark had asked the staff of the mission to give us the same bunk. He told me that way he could keep an eye out for me. He asked me if I had any valuables, such as a wallet. I innocently acknowledged that I did. He said he would protect it for me and return it in the morning. No one is truly safe in that environment. Many men removed their shoes and stored them under their pillows. Lessening the danger of having them stolen in the wee hours of the night supposedly grants the men a better night's sleep. As for me, I didn't sleep at all. In fact, it would be six weeks before a good night's sleep would fall upon me. It was one of many terrifying nights I would experience in the weeks to follow. The next morning, Mark returned my wallet. It was intact. I was told later that this was a highly unusual occurrence. Most people in my position would have been robbed, and possibly accosted. I was safe, and a new day waited.

Mark asked me what my plans for the day were. I told him someone suggested that I go to north Baltimore and see if I could get help from an organization called Teen Challenge. Before I could ask him how I could get there, he said that he would help me. He called a cab, and we started for the door. It was raining that October morning, and a chill breeze made me yearn to be anywhere but there. To this day, I marvel at God's provision for me. Mark took off his worn-out coat and grease-stained hat and offered them to me as shelter from the morning air. Our taxi came, and off we went to Teen Challenge.

As soon as we arrived, it was obvious that we were unwelcome visitors. After a brief encounter with the men sitting in the reception area, we were asked to leave. We walked out the door and onto the streets of Baltimore, a far cry from the streets of Edinburgh. My last hope had been no hope at all.

What took place over the next eight hours is somewhat of a blur to me. We walked, seemingly without direction. Without Mark, I would have dissolved into a crippling fear. On the streets you must keep your wits about you even if it's an illusion. The phrase "never let them see you sweat" never seemed so relevant. The day was an unending pursuit for shelter from the cold and rain, and for food of any description to fill our hollow stomachs. While our journey seemed aimless, Mark did know the city.

We eventually found a staging post where homeless people gather and are dispersed to shelters for the night. Homeless people seldom speak, not from lack of ability, but from the hopelessness of their situation. The staging area was filled to capacity. No one spoke, just blank stares. Whatever system there was for organizing the masses, it was not apparent to me. After about an hour, Mark grabbed my arm and said, "Let's go." Touching was not something the homeless did. It violates their space. So Mark's grabbing me was out of character for the situation, but it was something I needed very much. We walked across the street to the bus station and looked for a spot to nestle. Bus stations are not for nestling, but at that moment it was the best that Baltimore had to offer me. Mark said I would be safe here, and he went to the restroom, his coat and hat still protecting me. I sat there waiting for his return. It was a wait in vain. I never saw him again.

THESE WERE THE LONELIEST HOURS OF MY LIFE.

Without Mark's presence I was now petrified. These were the loneliest hours of my life. Sitting there in the corner, I searched my mind for options. There were none. I understood that if I died that night, I felt no one would even know where to send my remains. There was no one to call, no one to ask for help, no way to eat, nowhere to sleep. I sat there for hours contemplating my future. Finally I decided there was only one way I might survive the night. I walked across the street to the shelter staging area Mark had taken me to earlier. It had just closed. I pounded desperately at the door. Within moments, a woman came to the door and asked what I wanted. I explained my plight and asked if there was anything she could do to help me. All of a sudden another woman came into the room and inquired about my situation. She then asked me a question I will never forget, "Are you, by any chance, Mark Laurenson?" If I had arrived there earlier, I would have been swept away by the masses. If I had arrived any later, no one would have been there. I shudder to think what might have happened that night. But it didn't matter. I had shown up at the exact moment that God ordained.

Although I thought no one cared, I was wrong. Marie, my former wife, had called Warwick Manor just to check up on me. When she found out that I had been transferred to a facility in Baltimore, she continued her search. There she discovered my fate, a mission in the inner city. She panicked and began to search for me. To this day, she doesn't remember how it all unfolded. The miracle was that I had been found. The plan was to take me back to the mission where I was to spend the night. The next day Marie retrieved me and brought me back to Annapolis. Having done her part, she asked the men from my church to help me. My journeys were not over though, and perhaps the worse was yet to come.

What exactly do you do with a 56-year-old man who is homeless, broke, and a drug addict? To the leadership of the church there was only one solution, the world-renowned Pacific Garden Mission in Chicago. It had rescued many men from such a plight as mine, why not one more? Two days after my harrowing experiences on the Baltimore streets, I was given a one-way ticket to Chicago. I had now become like a cork bobbing to and fro in the sea. Exhausted and disoriented, I really had no option but to trust their judgment. The plan called for me to travel alone from Baltimore through the night, arriving in Chicago early Saturday morning. From there I was to take a cab to my future home. It had now been 16 days since I last slept. My ability to function at any level was almost depleted. That night on the bus defies description. All I knew was that my destiny was dark. I had lost all hope of surviving.

> I HAD NOW BECOME LIKE A CORK BOBBING TO AND FRO IN THE SEA.

Meanwhile back in Baltimore, Marie and her new husband, Tom, were growing increasingly concerned. Tom had grown up in Chicago and knew the Pacific Garden Mission for what it was, a homeless shelter in one of the most dangerous parts of the city. They spent the night trying to decide what to do. Once again Marie rose to the occasion. She and Tom determined that this was a disastrous plan. Arriving in Cleveland at 3 a.m., I struggled to find my transfer bus to Chicago. I must have looked like the lost puppy I was. A Greyhound employee asked if I was all right. I assured him that I was not. I was escorted to the ticket counter where I was once again asked, "Are you Mark Laurenson? If you are, your wife is on the line." I was overcome with emotion. How did she find me?

She told me that she and Tom had arranged for me to return to Baltimore on the next bus. With the help of some very kind Greyhound employees, I was given a free meal and placed on the right bus. I returned to Annapolis where Marie and Tom sheltered me in a local motel. But now what?

I barely remember the next week. Still suffering from a lack of sleep, I tried to regain some semblance of calm and direction. What was suggested to me I greeted with a good amount of skepticism – Teen Challenge in Harrisburg, Pennsylvania. Wasn't this the same organization I sought help from in Baltimore? And wasn't this program for teenagers? Marie asked me to call them and at least see if I could get more information. I did. One journey ended and another began.

> I ARRIVED VOID OF ALL HOPE, DEPRESSED, AND DESPERATELY NEEDING SLEEP.

Teen Challenge, as I found out, is an international organization started in New York City 40 years ago. Its initial focus was on gang members who needed redemption both spiritually and physically. It is a one-year residential program for men 17 and older who suffer from either alcohol or drug addiction. The induction phase is accomplished at one of a dozen sites throughout the country and around the world. Like Father Martin's, this phase lasts four months. Upon successful completion, you are sent to a second phase at a regional training center for your final eight months. The success rate is impressive. Taking a year out to focus on your spiritual and emotional health reaps outstanding results. A great program, I thought, but too drastic. At 56 and in poor health, a year of complete separation from friends and family sounded more like walking on hot coals with my bare feet than a solution for my problems. Nevertheless, in a matter of days, I left Annapolis for Harrisburg. I arrived void of all hope, depressed, and desperately needing sleep. The staff told me later that they felt I might not last the week, let alone a whole year.

The men of the Harrisburg induction center ranged from a 19-year-old convict to a 45-year-old executive. There was a professional wrestler, a master musician, and a college professor, men who had fallen from their mountaintops to men who had never even climbed out of the valley of their childhood. They were black, white, and Hispanic. It didn't matter who we were or where we came from, we were instantly brothers. I grew to love every single one of them. Well, almost!

I KNEW THAT GOD HAD NOT ABANDONED ME.

My time at Teen Challenge was difficult. Memories of having my life in Maryland severed so dramatically and the fear that the future was even bleaker were my constant companions. The physical pain that had introduced me to narcotics plagued me once again. But the care of the staff, the support of the men, and the growing understanding that God had not forsaken me awakened me from the darkness of my spiritual stupor. After months of Bible courses, Bible reading, and memorization, I realized anew that for a Christian there is no way of hanging on to our faith apart from significant time spent in both the Old and New Testament scriptures.

As the winter months passed, my life was restored. Since my addiction began more than a decade earlier, I had hope for the first time. I knew that God had not abandoned me. The joy of my salvation was being restored. But there was still the matter of the future. With no money in the bank and no monthly income, where would I live and how would I support myself? How easily my fears crowded in on my faith. You would have thought I'd become a giant of the faith by now. But I was still early in my "recovery" with many miles yet to be traveled.

The previous summer I had applied for disability through Social Security. Very few people ever get disability the first time around. On a Friday morning in late March I awoke, still wondering what my future held. That afternoon I received a call from the Social Security office telling me that I had been approved. Just one detail remained. Where did I want the check mailed? That night I went to sleep with a monthly income and a brand new bank account. Within weeks, an application for housing that I had submitted nine months earlier came through. I was finally getting the idea that God, for some unknown reason, had not only spared my life but was restoring me.

Why didn't I die in the auto accident? Why didn't I die from a drug overdose? Why didn't I have a terrible withdrawal from the narcotics in my system? Why did Mark protect me that night in the homeless shelter? Why did I come back to the staging area at just the right time? Why was Marie able to find me, not once but twice? Why, of all the drug facilities in the country, did I end up at Teen Challenge in Harrisburg? Why, at just the right time, was I given an income and a home? For me there is only one answer – the grace of God, the unmerited favor of God given to all who call out to Him in their time of need.

In Psalm 71, David looks back on his own life and reflects:

"Your righteousness reaches to the skies, O God,
You who have done great things,
Who, O God is like you?
Though you have made me see troubles, many and bitter,
You will restore my life again; from the depths of the earth
You will again bring me up.
You will increase my honor and comfort me once again."

This is my testimony. God has indeed done great things.

When I was a patient at Father Martin's Ashley, one of the exercises they asked us to do was to add up how much money our addiction had cost us. I sat there struggling to identify financial costs that had impacted my life. My drugs were obtained for a $10 co-pay. My job was intact, and I hadn't lost a car to the bank. I concluded that my addiction had had no financial impact on my life. Recently I revisited the issue. Including lost pay after losing my job, projected income to age 65, pension and health benefits, and the loss of my house due to my divorce, the grand total came to over one million dollars. It sounds high, even mind boggling, to contemplate my loss. But I stand in awe of what I have, the cleansing of my soul and the restoration of my life. I think I got a pretty good deal.

Chapter Five

The Ark
MY PLACE OF REFUGE

W ith an income secured through social security disability and my addiction to prescription drugs under control, it was now time to leave Harrisburg and return to Annapolis. Finding a home in an expensive area of the country such as Annapolis on a social security disability check was no easy matter, that is, unless God was working as your front man, leading the way. While still in Teen Challenge I received word that an apartment I had applied for ten months earlier was available. I saw it as God's provision, but I must be honest, I had prayed for something a little nicer.

To most people in Annapolis, 701 Glenwood was the address given to those less fortunate. Section 8 public housing, it was for the down and outers, those who couldn't make it in the real world, the poor, the disabled, those whose lives had taken broken trails on the way to their dreams if they had dreams at all. My reception at my home church had been less than warm. Except for the three folks who stayed in touch with me, most people still saw me as an active addict. I must admit, though, that I was probably overly sensitive. When people found out I was living in public housing, I felt even more like an outcast.

But God never fails, and He knew that 701 Glenwood was His provision in more than just one way. The people there knew that life could be hard, very hard! They were poor in money and in health, and many had no family at all to look to for support. But so many of them had what few people even in churches had – they had joy in their faith. It seems that many in desperate situations find a faith that is deep and open to all who will listen.

I LEARNED FROM STUDENTS THAT PEOPLE IN TROUBLE NEED TO HEAR FROM FOLKS WHO CAN RELATE TO THEIR STORIES WITH PASSION AND HUMOR.

Sunday morning was a visual treat. Reds and purples, oranges and yellows, and hats with flair! At first this violated my Presbyterian sensibilities, but I soon discovered a world of faith that transcended my limited cultural understandings. I learned a lot from them about the celebration of faith. I also learned a thing or two about helping the poor. Many churches have food pantries or soup kitchens. For the most part you must go to them. One church in particular rose to a new level. Mariners Church didn't wait for you to go to them. Once a year they descend upon Glenwood like locusts! Equipped with a semi-truck full of goods, the youth of the church, led by church leaders, brought to each apartment several large boxes of goodies, from food to footwear. They weren't content to just drop off the goods, but came with the idea of shaking hands, giving hugs and, of course, gently sharing their faith. Sinner and saved alike looked forward to their visits and spoke long afterward of their joy.

During my years after Teen Challenge I spent my productive time speaking at rehabs, youth groups, churches, and anywhere I was asked to come. I learned from students that people in trouble need to hear from folks who can relate to their stories with passion and humor.

My closest friend was Jim, a man in his late forties who had suffered a near fatal accident. After numerous surgeries he spent three years in rehab and had arrived at Glenwood about the same time as I did. He weighed more than 350 pounds and needed kidney dialysis three times a week. In short, he needed a new kidney, but he needed to lose 175 pounds to be considered for such a procedure. Jim was a product of faith in Jesus, and his spirit declared it. We had little in common. He liked NASCAR, I liked Indy Car. He had taught himself the intricacies of the computer, I could barely turn mine on. But we bonded and were always there for each other. I could tell you about so many others and their suffering. They were kind and welcomed me into their homes.

When it came to leave, I realized that 701 Glenwood, God's provision, had been my place of protection, my refuge, my asylum from the turbulent seas of life. It was my ark.

My brother Jim made his goal. He lost nearly 190 pounds. The day I left for Indiana he went in for final preparations leading to him get his new kidney. Several days later I got a call from his sister. Jim had had a massive heart attack on the operating table and was now with the Lord. I guess God knew His new

———

gifts to me meant Jim needed an even greater gift, a new body complete with working kidneys and a stroll with His master.

I thought Glenwood was just one more step downward. It turned out to be where I found new strength and unfolding belief that those who experienced the worst in life also saw the best. They saw Jesus.

Chapter Six

A Miracle Forty Years Delayed
MOVING ON AND LOOKING FORWARD

W hen it seems that God is no longer moving in your life, or at least His interest in you has waned, you may want to think again! Safe and secure living in the Ark, I had settled into a life that included a close group of friends and consistent activities at church. I could have maintained my relative comfort. But just when I thought I was retired from adventures, especially adventures of the heart, God broke into my world once again.

In early November 2009, my graduating class from Grace College celebrated its 40th reunion. Due to commitments at church and a lack of funds to make the trip, I was not able to attend. A week later a friend called to give me the highlights of the weekend and send a few photos. During our conversation he mentioned how my college sweetheart, my first love, had gone through some deep waters in her life, and after 30 years of marriage to a pastor, she was now divorced. I e-mailed her and simply said that I was deeply sorry for her troubles. I had no ulterior motives other than to share that I knew a thing or two about sorrow. I didn't really expect Robin to respond. At some

---

level, I didn't really care. I was too old and physically beat up to dream of something new in my life.

Robin did respond. At first we shared a few simple e-mails. By Thanksgiving the e-mails had turned to phone calls and by the first of the year the phone calls were the highlight of the week for both of us. While I enjoyed our new-found friendship, I determined to tell her all about my years of addiction and the ruin it brought to my family. Surely that would keep her from wanting a deeper relationship and I could stay in my comfortable rut! Besides, she deserved to know the truth.

I HAD DISCOVERED MY SOUL MATE.

I was wrong. To begin with, Robin had deep character and an amazing ability to love the unlovely. And second, I once again doubted God's working His wonders in my life.

Robin visited me in Annapolis in April of 2010, and we had a grand time. My friend Joel gave us a detailed and exclusive tour of the naval academy which we both enjoyed. By the end of the trip Robin and I were engaged. I had discovered my soul mate, and after many challenges in both our lives we could be together.

On July 3, 2010, less than a year from when we first reunited, Robin and I were married in Winona Lake, Indiana, where forty years earlier we had met. Our relationship had flourished in ways it never had when we dated in college. Who knows, if we had married earlier maybe we would not have connected the way we do now? Robin is just one more example of how perfect God's timing has been in my life.

Moving to Winona Lake was difficult and took the help of many friends and family members, but after 25 years in Annapolis it was time for a change. Robin's mother lived in a nursing home in Indiana and Robin had a job she loved working with medical records for a mental health facility. I couldn't ask her to leave that.

Life has gone on since God brought me through the trials of drug addiction. I toured churches speaking about addiction for years until my struggles with chronic pain ended that period of my life. Robin and I became active in our church and are continuing to grow together and with God. My relationship with my sons has begun to mend and they visit me often from their home in Nashville, Tennessee.

It would be a nice ending to the story to say I hadn't touched painkillers since my time in Teen Challenge, but that is not what happened. For seven years I was drug free, but in 2010 a serious fall on the ice brought chronic pain crashing back into my life. This time, however, I am going about pain management the healthy way. I have one doctor with whom I have signed a contract that prescribes my medicine unlike my days as an addict when I went to many different doctors to find drugs. The doctor and Robin know about my past and can keep me accountable for my drug use now while still aiding me in managing my pain.

In the spring of 2013 I had been reflecting on this telling of my story. I know it so well—it's accurate, and it's a work-in-progress. My primary goal was to help my boys understand my life journey, including the part their mother played in the story.

I searched my heart. What was my basic sin? I knew that having a stressful job and documented physical pain played a part, but that explanation didn't satisfy. I asked the Lord for insight, and He answered.

One of the turning points, I realized, was when my former wife had asked me to "just quit" my job. The strains at work were nearly unbearable, but I could not quit. I had gotten really accustomed to a six-figure income. I liked the lifestyle of five-star restaurants, staying in the nicest hotels, and having a certain status in the community. I was afraid to give it up.

MY SIN WAS THAT I JUST DIDN'T WANT TO TRUST GOD TO TAKE CARE OF US.

How would I find another job as generous? My sin was that I just didn't want to trust God to take care of us.

I began to realize some of the fears and insecurities that had plagued my ex-wife. Back then, Y2K was advancing toward us rapidly, and she had a strong fear about the future. She began to purchase rice and other supplies to prepare for the apocalypse. A small inheritance I had received was soon gone—mostly to purchase survival supplies. At her insistence we moved with a friend to the mountains of Pennsylvania, purchasing a gun with which to hunt for meat if necessary. She was so intent on moving that at one point she threatened that if I did not come along, "I'm taking the boys and I'm going."

Although my physical and emotional problems contributed to the breakup of the marriage, I now see clearly that my major sin was my refusal to trust God to take care of us in

---

uncertainty. I wasn't willing to give up the financial security we enjoyed, and so that "crutch" was removed from me by forces beyond my control.

What's next for Robin and me? As she nears retirement age we are keeping an open mind about the future. We might RV around the United States or maybe move to Nashville to be close to my sons and their families. One thing I know for sure: God led me through darkest times and blessed me by the night. He will lead me in the future.

FINAL THOUGHTS

I once felt that those whose lives were free of trouble were blessed of God. I no longer feel that to be the truth. James told us to "consider it all joy when troubles come your way." But what I don't believe is that we should purposely pursue troubles as though they make us spiritual. My battle with prescription drugs was self-induced. While God showed His grace time after time, it still wasn't a particularly good idea! It is important also to note that the reason we should treasure troubles is because they build our faith in God.

Troubles will come. Sometimes they will seem beyond our ability to overcome them. I hope some of the examples I have shared with you serve as an illustration of how God can make all things glorify Him, and just as importantly, build in us important recognitions:

FIRST: That God wants to share His grace with everyone. Remember, grace is God's unmerited favor. Unmerited favor, in a sense, is the message of the Gospel of Jesus Christ.

SECOND: The resulting product in our lives is character, the sum of the characteristics possessed by us all. It refers to our moral qualities and ethical standards. When our character is weak we seldom stand strong. When it is strong, we have an inner strength that comes from dealing with troubles.

I hope this journey through the darkest times of my life will shine a light on how amazing God's grace can be in your life as well. Troubles can be our friends and a sign that God is paying attention to us. Welcome them as the gift God intended them to be.

> *"Consider it pure joy, my brothers whenever you face trials of many kinds, because you know the testing of your faith produces steadfastness."*
>
> *James 1:2*

To testify is to give an eyewitness account of what we have seen with our own eyes. In Psalm 71, the Psalmist looks back on his own life and reflects:

> *"Your righteousness, O God,*
> *reaches the high heavens.*
> *You who have done great things,*
> *O God, who is like you?*
> *[20] You who have made me see many troubles and calamities*
> *will revive me again;*
> *from the depths of the earth*
> *you will bring me up again.*
> *[21] You will increase my greatness*
> *and comfort me again."*
>
> *Psalm 71:19-21 (ESV)*

LAURA STORY'S STORY

Most speakers, pastors, lecturers, teachers like to conclude their remarks with a poem, story, or song. I am one of those people! It is a good way to wrap up what they are trying to share with their audience.

I recently heard a song written and sung by Laura Story. It is a mirror of what I have offered in book form. Laura is a songstress who, as a fairly new bride, was confronted by the announcement that her husband had a brain tumor. It was not how she expected God to grant her a blessing.

In the song, Laura talks about how we pray for blessings and for peace, and for God to ease our sufferings. But God, who knows our need better than we do, often does not answer our prayers in the way we wish.

Although we often doubt His goodness and His love, Laura reminds us that all the while, God is listening and longing for us to have faith to believe. In the end, she marvels at a jolting "what if?"

It is just possible, she surmises, that some of life's greatest storms and trials are actually God's mercies in disguise. In her words:

> *"What if your blessings come through raindrops*
> *What if Your healing comes through tears*
> *What if a thousand sleepless nights are what it takes to know*
>   *You're near*
> *What if trials of this life are Your mercies in disguise."*

If you are interested in obtaining additional copies of Mark Laurenson's story, or in having him speak to a group, contact him at *marklaurenson@comcast.net* or write to him at:
Mark Laurenson
2340 S. Lake Sharon Rd.
Warsaw, IN, 46580